GEOGRAPHIES OF LIGHT

*

LISA SUHAIR MAJAJ

GEOGRAPHIES OF LIGHT

*

LISA SUHAIR MAJAJ

— DEL SOL PRESS • WASHINGTON D. C. —

DEL SOL PRESS, WASHINGTON, D.C.

Paper ISBN: 978-1-934832-08-0

First Edition

Cover photo courtesy Andreas N. Alexandou

Cover & Interior Design by Ander Monson

Publication by Del Sol Press/Web Del Sol Association,
a not-for-profit corporation under section 501(c)(3) of
the United States Internal Revenue Code.

CONTENTS

For Andros

Wise as you have become, with all your experience,
You will have understood the meaning of an Ithaka.
—Constantine P. Cavafy

REUNION

You'd think the dead would come at night:
shadows on a midnight wind,
shudders from the heart of mystery.

Instead they crowd in over my morning coffee,
hover insistently in the steam,
jostling their competing memories.

I tell them to come back later.
All those years of longing
and they think they can show up like creditors?

I have a family to feed, work to do.
But they are like petulant children
clamoring for attention.

My mother wants to give me
the cracked white porcelain angel
that stood on her dresser for years,

impervious to despair. I tell her *no*,
but she presses it into my hands.
While I'm pondering the pursed mouth,

the glue-stained wings, my father
pulls my t-shirt into a pouch,
fills it with clods of dry brown earth,

mumbling something about loss,
remembrance, Palestinian inheritance.
My uncle is next, holding

a glass of red wine to my lips.
On its surface I see faces
shimmering as if in a lake:

his wife, safe and whole before the bomb
that shook the East Jerusalem cobblestones
all those decades ago,

his sisters before the cholera epidemic,
his mother with a straight, young back.
He urges me to drink, but I fling the glass away,

hear it shatter on the tile.
My elderly aunt, our newest dead,
comes forward to sweep up the mess,

muttering about the carelessness
of the young. Ashamed,
I try to take the broom from her,

but she tells me to drink my coffee,
leave the dead to their own business.
When I raise the cup to my lips,

my mouth fills with dregs:
coarse, bittersweet, earth-dark,
dense as unclaimed memory.

HOMEMAKING

It was a place of stone and trees,
stooped houses slanting
into the road. Outside her window
workers chipped rough-hewn limestone

to blocks, staccato labor
splicing the air like rain.
What could she speak of?
Only the slow tick of light

across the floor, the chipped stone
of loneliness. Afternoons,
she watched shade drip
down the wall, collect in puddles

on the tile. Sometimes dusk found her
still there, ear pressed like a medic's
to the house's chiseled skin,
listening for the echo of her heartbeat,

for the measure of her life
in the faint settling of stone.

*

I was the child in the doorway, watching.
I was the child who saw her turn silently away.
I was the child who understood nothing.

I would be a pillow at the small of her back,
a glass of cold water on a tray,
a cloth shielding her from the sun.

I would be a dictionary
holding all the languages known and unknown.
I would save everything:

the space between moments,
the silence between words,
the sound of a door closing or opening.

*

She crossed an ocean and found a world
different and yet the same.
A woman's labor is a woman's labor.
It was enough, much of the time.

The birth pangs were another journey.
The tidal wave bore down,
left her storm-ravaged,
the child a beached animal on her belly.

Sometimes she felt her own life
flung up on herself
in just that way.
Once, slitting a pigeon for cooking,

underskin bloody beneath her knife,
she found a gleaming of eggs,
shells stark and tender
as infant moons.

She grieved, then, for her girls,
born to a world of men.

*

I see her in an unheated room at a piano,
door shut, too shy
to sing in a voice that might be overheard,

too lonely to remain silent.
I am outside, straining for the melody
that slips from the room

like the odor of baking bread.
Later she will move through the house
lit with a quiet light.

*

Once I woke early, birds were crying,
she was not in her bed.
I wandered through the house, searching,

summer tile cool beneath my feet.
Opening the front door, I saw her,
book in hand, robe crumpled loosely,

shoulders soft with the lingering touch
of sleep. At the sound of my step
she turned, the shine of privacy

still on her—a singular beauty,
like rain trembling on jasmine—
and composed herself to a smile.

TWO FLUTES

1.

Banyan trees patient as centuries.
Beirut barely stirring.
The Mediterranean luminous
with the expectation of light.

A redolence of salt.

Reem walked the path between pines,
brushed bougainvillea tremulous with rain.
Where she sat, cross-legged, stones shifted to hold her.

The air quavered,
nai coaxing rain to the sea,
birds to the air.

Each morning I listened for that swallow of sound,
that high sweetness.

2.

Summer held Amman in its breathlessness,
siesta of burning dust, sun melding to sky.

Construction chiseled the daze of heat,
shouts of laborers, swirl of stone dust,
weave of weariness, stone-chippers tapping
a blood rhythm.

Then tea-break—dusty voices subsiding
light chink of glasses

za'atar pungent, steeping—
and from that hush

a single *nai*

deliquescence of labor
        a high keening

3.

Even fleeing Lebanon
boat slipping out of Jounieh into a ravaged dusk

gunboats ringing the harbor
flares stitching sky to a crumbling horizon

that melody threaded the dark

a clear space
        widening

4.

I have been searching since

the seven hills of Amman
white stone wealth of mansions
fading into an impossible blue dusk
moon choking the sky with its radiance

for a high note
        trembling

WHAT SHE SAID

They don't have snow days in Palestine, they have military invasion days.
—International Solidarity Movement activists, describing Palestinian
children's lives under occupation.

She said, go play outside,
but don't throw balls near the soldiers.
When a jeep goes past
keep your eyes on the ground.
And don't pick up stones,
not even for hopscotch.
She said, don't bother the neighbors,
their son was arrested last night.
Hang the laundry, make the beds,
scrub that graffiti off the walls
before the soldiers see it. She said,
there's no money; if your shoes
are too tight, cut the ends off.
This is what we have to eat,
we won't eat again until tomorrow.
No, we don't have any oranges,
they chopped down the orange trees.
I don't know why. Maybe the trees
were threatening the tanks. She said,
there's no water, we'll take baths next week,
insha'allah. Meanwhile, don't flush the toilet.
And don't go near the olive grove,
there are settlers there with guns.
No, I don't know how we'll harvest
the olives, and I don't know what we'll do
if they bulldoze the trees. God will provide
if He wishes, or UNRWA, but certainly not
the Americans. She said, you can't
go out today, there's a curfew.
Keep away from those windows,
can't you hear the shooting?

No, I don't know why they bulldozed
the neighbor's house. And if God knows,
He's not telling. She said,
there's no school today,
it's a military invasion.
No, I don't know when it will be over,
or if it will be over. She said,
don't think about the tanks
or the planes or the guns
or what happened to the neighbors.
Come into the hallway,
it's safer here. And turn off that news,
you're too young for this. Listen,
I'll tell you a story so you won't be scared.
Kan ya ma kan—there was or there was not—
a land called *Falastine*
where children played in the streets
and in the fields and in the orchards
and picked apricots and almonds
and wove jasmine garlands for their mothers.
And when planes flew overhead
they shouted happily and waved.
Kan ya ma kan. Keep your head down.

I REMEMBER MY FATHER'S HANDS

because they were large, and square
fingers chunky, black hair like wire

because they fingered worry beads over and over
(that constant motion, that muted clicking, that secular prayer)

because they ripped bread with quiet purpose
dipped fresh green oil like a birthright

because after his mother's funeral they raised a tea cup
set it down untouched, uncontrollably trembling

because when they trimmed hedges, pruned roses
their tenderness caught my breath with jealousy

because once when I was a child they cupped my face
dry and warm, flesh full and calloused, for a long moment

because over his wife's still form they faltered
great mute helpless beasts

because when his own lungs filled and sank they reached out
for the first time pleading

because when I look at my hands
his own speak back

OLIVE TREES

We drive between rows of olive trees
that lean into the road like ghosts,
silver-green under the moon of midnight,
and remember spreading sheets on dry earth,
knocking branches till the hard fruit fell,
the glisten of hands smeared with oil.

A single tree stands watch outside our window.
All night long its roots hold the earth.

Now we walk out into the tunnel of days
and a million memories rustle:
waves that touch the shore and whisper,
touch the shore and whisper,
till we bend to gather them
and they flow through our fingers
leaving only a glaze of salt.

My daughter knuckled her way down the birth canal, emerging as if from an ancient cave: eyes wide, brow furrowed at what she had witnessed. She had no words, just a cry echoing from the deep almond-shaped eyes that held my gaze insistently, daring me to look away. Where she had come from only minutes before, not one of us could go and she could not return. Did she know this, those first few minutes on my chest, her face still slimed with the mucus of birth? She came headfirst into a space of music, Fairuz singing *Jerusalem in My Heart*, safely delivered, as they say, as if she were a parcel that might have gotten lost en route, but instead had reached its final destination. We were both delivered, I of her and she of me, and thus we each ended one journey and started another, spinning with the planet's centrifugal whirl. We have been traveling ever since, at times in opposite directions, and often the only evidence I have of our common origins is the odor of almond clinging to her hair.

I am asked, do I hope she will one day return to Palestine, to the United States, to Cyprus, to any of her points of origin? I think of lines on a map, the blue spaces we traverse with a single flight, the world so small that sometimes it seems we will all be swallowed by proximity, so large that we can never encompass its vastness. Behind every symphony is its origin point: a space redolent with silence. I look at myself in the mirror, I who am fractured at the core, yet whole inside my skin and in my heart. Behind my reflection I catch a glimpse of my daughter swimming, sun glinting off every wave. She will grow in her body, travel where she wishes, love whomever she chooses. And when she returns it will be to her own whole heart.

DOORWAY

The distance between one breath and another
is like the miles starlight travels to reach

my dreams. I write my way toward my death,
behind me a crumb trail of words erasing,

birds carrying morsels to their hungry chicks.
Years I've traveled the byways

of language, searching for that doorway—
light spilling over the threshold.

Voices murmur beneath sleep,
weave a sky dense with memory.

Once a poet read lines so beautiful
I knew I could follow her down

the hardest road without faltering.
My feet grew tired, but I remembered my name.

PROVENANCE

I come from olive and oleander,
from pistachio, almond and fig,
from the many tendrils of vine.

I come from light, strong and splintered,
from the *khamsin* browning the sky,
from walls of gentled stone chiseling a face.

I come from a scraped knee, a bloody palm,
from trees climbed and fences scaled,
from the metallic whir of roller skates across tile.

I come from dust and smoke,
from the bleating of butchered animals
and the spiny silence of cactus.

I come from the hum
of a woman walking a floor
with a sleepless child,

crooning an off-key melody,
tender undertones
filling the dark,

till the moon rises,
the night opens,
and all the stars shine out.

MORNING

It's the clock at 5 a.m.
crust of light peeled back
quarried stone of insomnia

it's chunks of day
slashed from the bone of night
bloodied on the butcher's block

it's the stack of dreams
piled up like broken plates
regret pulled up like a muddy quilt

it's the cicadas that fly in your face
with rasping wings
chanting every phoneme in your name

POPPIES

what longing thrust me into the wind
searching for poppies
as if they could save me?

they wouldn't last: a week,
maybe two, and exuberant earth
would be muted, a gift retaken

I'd need to depend on memory

smooth taste
of sun
those brilliant cries

those red-tongued mouths
wild
with surprise

so I hoard memories
sort them for seeds to plant
pray they root

pine shrubs
on stony slopes
blossoms startling a hill

fierce tongues beneath transient skies
those stars of imploding songs
those poppies now

AMMAN, 1970

and when the shooting lulled
my father ran out the back door
to scatter chicken feed

we peered through the kitchen window
as the chickens pecked for grain
beaks glinting like shrapnel

shells littered the yard

no eggs all fall

TAPROOT

Once she could have held anything steady
and safe: a glass of tea, her brother's baby.
Now her hands shake at the weight of a fork.

Yet neighbors still come to her for cuttings
and she shows them how to let a stem breathe
in water, settle soil around branching roots.

*

After exile she built a house in the new place.
With years the stone walls browned like summer skin.
In her garden, peaches clustered like moons.

Uprooted, any stalk or vine
would whither and die. But if the taproot
is strong, a transplant can live.

*

What she knows is a kernel of darkened sun.
She could tell you how soldiers bulldozed trees,
smashed wells, how exposed roots shrivel.

Lifting jars of oil in the kitchen
(rich sustenance from bitter fruit)
her hands tremble with the weight they bear.

*

Sometimes, mounding dirt around new transplants
in the garden, she pauses—
fists knuckling, tenacious roots, into the earth.

TATA OLGA'S HANDS

My grandmother's hands were brown as the eggs she boiled in onion skins for Easter, rough like the bark of the jasmine vine that twined its way up the back wall of her chipped-stone house. She ladled *maftoul* in steaming portions, chick peas and onions afloat in the gold-brown sauce, hands firm as she hefted the bowl from stove to table. Tomato in one hand, knife in the other, rivulets ran to her wrists. The bread was paper thin and tore in long strips, dusting her hands with flour. Afterwards she poured tea over mint leaves, stirred a spoon round and round till the sugar dissolved, offered the steaming glass.

When my uncle died, *Tata* Olga washed his body with a stained white rag, wrung the cloth out fiercely in clear cool water. In the kitchen bitter coffee boiled in a huge pot over an open flame. Her knuckles were white on the ladle. She carried the tray without wavering, offered tiny cups that mourners tilted between thumb and forefinger. Cigarette smoke hung on the air. All evening she held out her palms.

Summer days on the farm, sun high in the languid sky, air so still a body could almost hear the corn growing, the two girls crawled beneath the fence, scrambled down the slope through tall grass till they reached the place where mosquitoes hummed and cowslip grew along the creek.

Once there, they shucked off shoes, held dresses high above their knees as they entered cool dark water, feeling their way through ripple and rivulet over packed dirt slippery to the step. Patches of cooler depths gave way to sun-warm shallows, bullfrogs grunting from the reeds, till water widened over sand and butterflies hovered like yellow flakes.

By then their dresses were already wet, so they laughed and splashed each other and slapped the water to hear the smacking sound. Sometimes they lay down amid the minnows, arms and legs undulating like cloud shadows, and pretended to swim. Other times they crouched in the slew, conjuring landscapes from promontories of mud (capes, peninsulas, fiords, bays, beaches—coastal scenes from an inland girl's dreams) till sun sank low in the sultry sky and they knew their mother would be calling. Then they smoothed their wet skirts, wiped the mud from their faces, and clambered up the hill to supper.

Years later, one of them would travel to one hundred seventeen countries on seven continents of the spinning globe, while the other would make her life in a place her neighbors knew only from church-tales of the Holy Land. Each would journey more miles in a year than their immigrant forbears had traversed in a lifetime. They would eat strange foods and watch the sun set over landscapes so far from the family farm that it was easy to think they'd never reach home again. But if anyone had told them this then, they'd have laughed, for no matter how far a-field imagination took them, they always ended up back at the farmhouse, tiptoe at the kitchen sink, rinsing creek water off their arms.

It's not that I want to change their lives, transfix them in that moment between day and dark, afternoon winding down, potatoes frying on the stove for supper, cats weaving around their feet as they giggled softly about the long day's playing. I just want to believe in a time when afternoon stretched out forever: when there was always a tomorrow rolling up, long and languid and innocent as the creek flowing cool and promising over childhood feet.

In memory of Jean and Marian Stoltenberg

She has a look beyond answer:
skin torn and ravaged, welts bloodied
by her desperate hands. Stained
cotton gloves offer scant
protection. Asleep, her hands
rip her flesh, tear blindly
at the bone-deep itch.
Mornings, she soaks bloody sheets
in cold soapy water.

One doctor calls her *hysterical housewife*,
prescribes sedatives. Others shrug.
"Dermatitis. We can't do much."
She tries every home remedy
she hears of, bathes in brews
of artichoke flowers, smears on
thick layers of cream—
something different each week.

This is before she sees the oncologist.
Before her hair falls out, body swelling
in inverse proportion to hope.

*

"Olive oil soothes the skin,"
someone tells her. Wearily,
she brings the half-filled flask,
lays herself open on the bed.
At the sight of her body
my breath clogs—skin bruised purple,
welts crusted with blood.
I look away from this last privacy
surrendered. My hands—hesitant,

27

ashamed—spread green oil thickly
over fragile skin, smooth torn flesh gently.

I long for the laying on of hands,
some touch weaving light between us.
But she doesn't ask for miracles.

*

After her mother died she bore me,
small seed of flesh—*new heart*—
into sheltering light.

Daily she caught my hair in tight braids,
hands cool and strong, gathered strands
like memories. She taught me the games
of childhood, called me *pumpkin, sweet pea*,
drew me—rumpled, whole—into my life.

*

My hands, blind fish,
feel their way across the body
that bore me. She is the child
I do not yet have, the mother
I have already lost,
the friend I cannot heal.

I reach for some faith
to gather us. There is only
this weave of love:

grieving hands, torn
flesh, dense oil smoothed
between us like light.

SEA BONES

Before my mother died, she confessed,
"My body's gone bad on me."
Her hands, delicate fins,

curved an arc of despair.
Days later, she sank
before the morning light

had fully washed in.
I cast out net after net,
came up with a litter of shells,

empty and salt-crusted.
At the shore there's only
the fierce crescendo

of waves. What we cast out
as anchor returns,
fragments of bone in our nets,

hard white *glossa*—tongue
of the squid, curl of calcium
left after sea strips flesh.

It's an old fisherman's secret:
ground to white powder, *glossa*
staunches the bleeding of wounds.

THE PAST

smells like afternoon rain
cumin and coriander
stone dust and cactus flowers

shines like a cooking pot
or a fresh-combed braid
a-swing down an ironed dress

rings with love songs and radio static
boredom and blackouts
bizir and backgammon and dice

drifts with sawdust and sunlight
bent wire and bullets
bubbling tar on a summer roof

reeks of gunpowder and garbage
candles and kerosene
spoiled meat and flat warm beer

lilts with lemon and laughter
ashtrays and prayer-beads
lipstick and lavender

smolders—a book
left too near the fire
crumbling at a touch

IN SEASON

My father knew the weight of words
in balance, stones in a weathered wall.

He counseled patience,
though, dying, refused his own advice.

Today his words surround me
with the quiet intensity of growing things,

roots planted a long time ago
lacing the distances of my heart.

What he didn't say is sprouting too,
a surprise, like the *eskidinya* tree

that sprang from the smooth brown pit
I tossed off the porch as a child.

Years now I've longed to pick that fruit,
remembering how he'd sit

spitting seeds in a stream to the ground.
But I know it's not yet ripe.

So I think instead of the lemon tree
in my uncle's yard. When it died,

no one could bear to cut it down.
They lopped off the branches

but kept the dead trunk, stumps
of arms upraised: each bearing,

like bird's nests, a potted plant.
Out of habit, they still water the trunk,

and as if in return, each branch sparks green—
though every heart's separate, now,

not like the lemons that used to cluster
like triple suns. Did my parents know

that what they planted,
roots against the drought,

would survive? Today,
I'm a stump of a branch.

Yet on my tongue a seed
lies dormant, dense with life.

Unspoken years
fill my mouth like citrus

in winter—sharp promise
of sun. Outside, *eskidinya*

hang heavy as memory,
orange flash from dusty leaves,

their season still ripening.

◄ III ►

POMELO DAYS

January
rain jewelling the jasmine
dark blossoming early

my father pushed the door open
arms filled with rustling sacks
winter clinging to his collar

poured out great yellow rounds of pomelo
dimpled like grapefruit, but pear-shaped
seeds dense as teeth

and sure as the rain in winter
we knew
pomelo days had come

STONE FENCE

I was a small child climbing walls, defying my father's injunctions.
Who wants a tomboy for a wife? I clambered up cherry trees,
skinned my knees, rode my bike farther than I was allowed
to go. On picnics I collected rocks, hoarding them in the old tin can
I kept under my bed. It rattled like my mother's button box.

My father planted jasmine, watered rosebushes. My mother
weeded the strawberry patch, picked berries, juice staining
her mouth and hands. My grandmother gathered *ba'elli*
from the garden, boiled Easter eggs in onion skin, fasted
two weeks each year in gratitude that her baby, my father, had lived.

That was years ago. Now they're gone, all of them. Chinks
in me fill with voices like green things sprouting, wisps of life
between rocks. Birds drop seed, soil collects in pockets.

I tilt toward the earth, leaning with the weather, held
in place by little more than gravity and the tenacious will
of someone who gathered stones from the field, placing them
one atop another, trying to make something that would stay.

From how many lives? I build myself up as I go.

IN THE WOODS

There is so much to carry, though we try
to strip down. Tents, sleeping bags, tarps,
stoves, cups, bowls, maps, band-aids.
Keep it light, the guide says. We try.

We are still learning the basics.
How to layer socks inside boots,
wool thick and fragrant around raw flesh.
How to load the pack, balance the weight,
readjust the straps. How to walk, top-heavy,
cumbersome, sure each step will send us crashing
down the mountain. How to pitch the tent
in a downpour, start a fire with wet wood,
purify water from the stream.
How to get the gear back into the stuff sack,
hoist the pack, balance the weight,
start walking again, one foot before the other,
a movement steady and slow as breathing.

It sounded easy, this walking into the woods,
searching for what got lost:
ground resilient beneath our feet, sky glimmering
between branches of trees older than any of us.
We wanted to remember how to live.
Instead, we barricade ourselves behind our packs,
the things we can't do without.
We speak of the blisters on our feet,
not light rippling across wet green leaves.

*

Some people walk into the woods
with nothing but a knife in their hands
and the clothes on their back.

There is a woman who does this each fall,
counting on her strength and skill for survival,
on what the forest offers of food and shelter:
animals yielding flesh and skin,
roots twisting in matted earth,
a twig holding fire in its dark, wet heart.

What does she think about, alone for months,
each day a project of food and warmth,
the forest swallowing her whole over and over?
Imagine setting down a lifetime
at the edge of the woods where the trees
start to thicken. That old rock in your chest
thrown down. The echo of your solitary voice
a snowflake in the imagination of winter.

OAK

She took her slice of life
then gave without measuring
or counting

something for everyone
extra for those
who understood her gifts too late

I'd like to think she kept some for herself
but if a crumb remained
she'd feed the birds first, chuckling with pleasure

She carried stories in her head
a pencil in her pocket
laughter in her eyes

and in her heart
the determination
of an immigrant's daughter

When she visited sorrow
she kept it short
and always came back smiling

Maybe her heart was just too large for her body
and so had to burst free
flames breaking from a twisted oak

That last moment,
turning to speak,
breath catching in her throat

did she remember sunlight
daffodils, garlic
the redolence of worn shoe leather?

Years before, a boy and a girl
each set out on the journey
to the new world

Whatever it cost them to exchange
one country for another, they paid it
and in the new place they found each other

Perhaps on the day of her birth
they looked down at her waving fists
smiled across at each other and nodded

this one's a fighter

In memory of Evelyn Abdallah Menconi

THE SHOES

are scattered in disarray, as if kicked off tiredly
at the end of the day; one overturned by the bed,
another peering out beneath the bookshelf.
Expensive leather, smooth to the touch, still radiates

the aura of life, warmth of the feet that tapped impatiently
under desks, took stairs two at a time, strode, impetuous,
down vibrant sidewalks—that walked out the door
that last morning, confident of return. Now they lie

like shadowed footprints. Gravely I lift them from the ground,
settle them in their shoe box, tentatively close the lid—
as if they might protest, leap from their resting place,
stamp furiously out the door, reclaim the bustling avenues

and all their riches. But they lie motionless in their shroud
of tissue. I switch off the light, close the closet door, confront
the silent room: pants drooping across a chair, shirt flung
across the exercise bike, hats stacked like dusty ghosts on the ledge.

From outside the window comes a faint tapping—
footsteps of the living as they go about their business.

In memory of Faris Bouhafa

BEIRUT, 1982

tilting walls careen
sliced edges collide
    with harsh flat planes of sky

gray dust billows
    from rubble
        raw flesh of buildings
    ripped from steel bones
            twisted
            maimed

sun bleeds into gray light

    behind web-cracked hospital glass
a taut man   grimed with stubble
contours of eyes torn hollow
    clutches a child   limp rag
        of bones   and blood
            a steady splatter
        onto swabbed tile floors

    gunfire
                a stacatto

        drumming

DEPARTURE

Every time I think of leaving, my heart wrinkles.
—Samira Atallah

Leaving is always
like this. Years
of hours and days
ticked off like
a body count:
what's left but
shards of memory
smoothed and hoarded,
shrapnel griefs,
a few regrets?
It should be simple
to leave: land falling
away like fear,
old skylines erasing.

But lines etched
into skin after years
of weather
chart boundaries
we cannot cross:
tangles of blood ties,
history's scars,
love's tide-lines of salt.

After leave-takings
planned and unplanned,
deaths we're forced
to move on from,
we learn these things:
how to say goodbye
quickly, how to choose

what to take when
we go, how to live
without what we leave
behind. We learn
to like empty spaces,
blank walls, shadowless
light; to pour loss
like coarse salt
through our fingers.

Some things remain:
light no one can capture,
voices that sing alone,
the touch of snow on air.

Some seeds planted
in brine still grow.

Who knew the past would follow us so far,
years collapsing like an ancient accordion,
scraps of memory tucked like torn photographs
into the sockets of our eyes?

Remember the gray Beirut seafront, car pulling up,
men ordering, "Get in," our hearts thudding against bone
as we broke and ran? Remember the splintered staccato
of bullets against rock, the way dust rose
in the stunned aftershock of silence?

Days were punctuated by static and news,
nights by the brilliance of tracer bullets
in flight. We huddled on campus steps,
transistor radios pressed to our ears,
straining for some echo of the future.

That day we finally fled the beleaguered city
(tanks rolling in, danger a promise waiting
patiently) the sun sank blazing behind us
into the sea, marking a trail of blood-red light:
a path offering return.

But return was a story scribbled in a notebook
misplaced during flight. We journeyed far,
exchanged one country for another,
survived one war to live a lifetime within
others. We learned to let our faces hide
our selves, to speak our story in a private
tongue, the past a shadow in our bones.

Salt water and sojourns leave their traces.
Decades later we hoard echoes,
still breathe the dust of that place
where banyan trees tangle
in the earth, gesticulate toward light.
Fragments of memory welter
in our flesh, fierce
and penetrating as shrapnel.

For Andros

SEASONS OF FIRE, SEASONS OF LIGHT

Outside Lebanon, New Hampshire
a hundred trees are chanting of fall.
When the wind stirs, gold coins flash
under every tongue. Their fares have been paid,
but the dead still can't cross
to the other side. Bright ghosts, they linger
on the chill New England air.

*

We're still traveling the road from Beirut.
Still remembering how blossoms trembled
in gold clouds on the trees
the morning of evacuation.
We leaned out from the truck, grasped branches,
clung till petals stripped off in our hands—
delicate flakes that stuck a long time
to our sweaty palms.

From the sea, refugees watched constellations erupt,
fire searing the coast. All night the stars imploded.
We fingered amulets into the long future:
the ones who were lost.

*

Here, leaves flare from dark wood,
incandescent. A thousand tongues unfurl
into flame, swirl orange smoke to the sky.
Sumac glows, maple breathes fire.

Come winter, skeletons will grid the sky.
After the brilliance of autumn,
nothing will be clearer than the simplicity of loss.

But a hidden current runs
through the branches, sparks
to green flame come spring.

*

In Besharri, the cedars stand watch,
green and steadfast. Years plant themselves,
seeds sprouting from cracks
in the rock above rushing torrents:
Nahr Qadisha Blessed River,
Nahr Nabaat River of the Springs.
Lebanon's hills enfold all the dead,
known and unknown. Memory trickles
down limestone in steady rivulets,
watering the vines that bear fruit,
the trees whose roots lace the mountain.

When the war stilled, bulldozers clearing rubble
found ancient ruins beneath the streets,
forgotten histories brought to vision.
Everything lost continues:
a star's light streams past its dying,
ripples widening beyond grief.

*

Now autumn is moving further south.
Sumac and dogwood and burningbush
crest the hills in brilliant waves.
Sassafras and sweetgum fill the hollows.

At *mahrajans*, immigrant melodies
coaxed from an *oud* or *nai*
flow across oak leaves and open spaces,
the way light moves through water
or a voice trembles with memory.
Listeners hum and sway, clap hands
or slip into dance. They know what joy costs,
how knives hollow wood to this resonant
shell. Sojourners, they've paid the fare.
They want musicians' hands flashing
like larks, notes rippling in clear
light strains, roads opening toward the sea.

*

In Lebanon, spring comes early,
almond trees whitening to mist
in the sea's soft breath. Dawn
sparks blossoms of dew to crystal.
Buds break, tongue to green flame.

Travelers rising early to check the weather
find the hills taken by fire.

IT WASN'T POETRY

It wasn't poetry, those days
(summer toothsome as a ripe fruit
juice dripping down our wrists)

It was trees and shadows
pieces of wind blown in from the sea
boats and waves and bodies

It was the full moon
yellow as a smoker's tooth
red palms pressed against the sky

It was voices climbing atop each other
like crazed people in a locked room
a child's wail pulled from a private place

It was moonlight pooling on the concrete
long oars of light
the silver odor of blood

It was sentinels falling
dregs of desperation
ceasefire seizing the streets

and the future
lifetimes away
dreaming us safe

IV

GUIDELINES

If they ask you what you are,
say Arab. If they flinch, don't react,
just remember your great-aunt's eyes.

If they ask you where you come from,
say Toledo. Detroit. Mission Viejo.
Fall Springs. Topeka. If they seem confused,

help them locate these places on a map,
then inquire casually, Where are you from?
Have you been here long? Do you like this country?

If they ask you what you eat,
don't dissemble. If garlic is your secret friend,
admit it. Likewise, crab cakes.

If they say you're not American,
don't pull out your personal,
wallet-sized flag. Instead, recall

the Bill of Rights. Mention the Constitution.
Wear democracy like a favorite garment:
comfortable, intimate.

If they wave newspapers in your face and shout,
stay calm. Remember everything they never learned.
Offer to take them to the library.

If they ask you if you're white, say it depends.
Say no. Say maybe. If appropriate, inquire,
Have you always been white, or is it recent?

If you take to the streets in protest,
link hands with whomever is beside you.
Keep your eye on the colonizer's maps,

geography's twisted strands, the many colors
of struggle. No matter how far you've come, remember:
the starting line is always closer than you think.

If they ask how long you plan to stay, say forever.
Console them if they seem upset. Say, don't worry,
you'll get used to it. Say, we live here. How about you?

GROUND SPACE

Amman to Jerusalem
is miles, and not just of earth.
Even air space is enemy
territory—no telephone wire,
no power or wisdom can bridge
this gap. If I were there
we would be enemies, each
to a side, knowledge obscured
in these twisting hatreds.
Instead, I mourn, wonder what
I could say to you anyway,
what you might say to me.

Memory's the thing
they say you own but I've
made up. I lie awake nights,
seared by images: flecks of ash
swirling, the millions dead.
But other memories smolder,
burn: razed groves of orange
and olive, forced marches,
children broken and dying,
homes sealed and leveled,
bones snapped like a curse.

Each year a solemn hope,
a subtle despair: *next year
in Jerusalem.* A common
memory, a common dream.

*

When I come to Jerusalem
—the line barring east from west

invisible, palpable—
will we walk steep dusty roads
to neat parlors, balance cups
on our knees, peel ripe figs
from the garden?
If we drink coffee, we might tell
fortunes in the grounds, dark
like earth, a thumbprint
marking each claim
to the future. Each cup
will be different, the patterns
emphatic or faint, the futures
complex or clear: each
with its pool of darkness—anger
or pain—unless drifts of birds
bring calm. Ridges and whorls
of each print etch hopes
for peace: hand clasped in hand
firmer than fist on a gun
or club, hand raised in greeting
stronger than hand raised to strike.

We might plant together, pluck
grapes, brew coffee, tell new
fortunes each day, wash away
grounds of anger. History could be
this simple: earth—the final
claim—cupped like sunlight.

All we need
is ground space.

Amman, 1988

OUT-OF-STATE

The clerk says, "I need to see some ID."
She shrugs, starts digging
through her scuffed brown leather bag.

She's got wiry hair, olive skin,
eyes glinting dark and intense—
in his view, clearly not local.

She hands him a passport:
picture inside, family name,
all the particulars

that would pull her out of line
in another place. He peers
at strange stamps, fluid text,

reads out loud: "Place of birth—
Palestine." *A land
with no borders, too many maps.*

She's waiting, resigned—
it's obvious she's done this before.
He's flipping pages, brow furrowed.

Finally he looks up,
shakes his head brusquely.
"Sorry, no out-of-state

passports accepted here."
No out-of-state passports!
She's got too much dignity to argue,

or even laugh. But as I watch her
walk out, head held high,
I picture that state, still dream

and desire, its slopes green
with olives—trees patient and unyielding
as memories of earth.

TATA BAHIYEH

For that generation

Tata Bahiyeh was light
in the bones and older
than anyone: hands stained
with brown spots, flesh
so dry it folded
in ridges. Her touch
was like jasmine
flowering at night,
secret life slow
through the tough brown vine.

Bahiyeh loved apricots,
sun's fruit, rivulets
sweet down her storied
skin. The pits she spat
in her palm were a promise,
not to be wasted. Cracked,
you could eat the firm
white heart within. Planted,
seed pledged to grow.

Bahiyeh was like all
the old ones, longing
for earth and the light
off *Al-Aqsa*, olive trees
rooted on hills—prayers
under breathing. Their eyes
were pathways, marked out
and empty: at least
to be buried there,
earth cradling bones
in a final planting.

Like all of them,
she tucked packets
of tissue-wrapped seeds
(each with its story)
in drawers, behind
clocks, on shelves:
to plant in the better time,
insha'allah. Meanwhile,
travelers eastward
brought cuttings, sprigs
in the luggage: olive
and plum, bitter orange
and sweet black grape.

*

She didn't want much
in death, just a place
to rest. She was lucky,
had the papers, could cross.
But when Bahiyeh died,
the soldiers dumped her body
without ceremony
on the concrete floor,
probed roughly
into sheltered crevices
of her stiffened corpse.
They expected contraband,
money, munitions,
anything but death.
They found
what they should
have expected.

What light
remained in her bones
still beyond desecrating hands
shone hidden
and private.

*

When you look,
you find seeds, dusty
and shriveled,
brown shells fragile
like ancient bones.
You remember
how to lay kernels
in earth, pour water,
wait for the green
shoot thrusting,
amazed how seeds
harbor their light
within. Bahiyeh's bones
lie buried in girlhood
soil. You watch for
that steady emanation
of light. You learn
how to wait
after planting.

GRIEF-GHOSTS

They drift through the bedroom, the study, the hall,
pallid and thin like the wraiths that they are.

I'd like to fatten them up as my mother would have done,
nourish and care for them, stoke them a layer of fat

against the cold. (Never mind that my mother is among them;
this time I'll feed her.) So I tell them

to come, warm themselves at the fire, eat.
Fantasies are as popular with the dead

as with the living. Soon they're clustered in my kitchen,
clamoring for handouts. I know I can't rescue them

from their fate, stave off that moment when they'll fade
back to ghost land. My tears will be useless,

except to salt the food. But still I settle them at the table,
serve up huge portions, urge them to eat. Bodiless, they go along,

ask for seconds, joke about my cooking. I know they're only doing it
to humor me, but this is a game we're all playing—

grief-ghosts, each one of us. They need me to stay alive
and I need them to keep from dying.

RECOGNIZED FUTURES

Turning to you, my name—
this necklace of gold, these letters
in script I cannot read,
this part of myself I long
to recognize—falls forward
into my mouth.

You call my daily name, *Lisa*,
the name I've finally declared
my own, claiming a heritage
half mine: corn fields silver
in ripening haze, green music
of crickets, summer light sloping
to dusk on the Iowa farm.

This other name fills my mouth,
a taste faintly metallic,
blunt edges around which my tongue
moves tentatively: *Suhair*,
an old-fashioned name,
little star in the night. The second girl,
small light on a distanced horizon.

Throughout childhood this rending split:
continents moving slowly apart,
rift widening beneath taut limbs.
A contested name, a constant
longing, evening star rising mute
through the Palestine night.
Tongue cleft by impossible languages,
fragments of narrative fractured
to loss, homelands splintered
beyond bridgeless rivers,
oceans of salt.

*

From these fragments I feel
a stirring, almost imperceptible.
In the morning light these torn
lives merge: a name on your lips,
on mine, softly murmured,
mutely scripted, both real
and familiar, till I cannot
distinguish between your voice
and my silence, my words
and this wordless knowledge,
morning star rising
through lightening sky,
some music I can't quite
hear, a distant melody,
flute-like, *nai* through
the olives, a cardinal calling,
some possible language
all our tongues can sing.

The audience watches curiously
as the Arab-American woman steps up
to the podium. Light hair and skin,
unaccented English…they thought
she'd be more—you know—*exotic*.

Or: the audience waits attentively
as the Arab-American woman steps up
to the podium. She is cousin, compatriot,
fellow-traveler, Arab resonance
in a place far from home.

The Arab-American woman hesitates.
She's weary of living on only one side
of the hyphen. Her poems aren't just translations.
But if she blinks, someone always cries out,
Look at those Arab eyes!

She longs to walk into the forest empty handed,
climb up a mountain and down again,
bearing no more than what any person
needs to live. She dreams of shouting from
a high place, her voice cascading down

wild rivers. Already she can hear the questions:
"Do Arab women do things like that?"
And the protests: "We have so many problems!
—our identity to defend, our cultures under siege.
We can't waste time admiring trees!"

The Arab-American woman knows who she is,
and it's not what you think. She's authentic
in jeans or in an embroidered dress.

When she walks up a mountain, her identity
goes up with her and comes back down again.

Besides, she's learned a secret.
Two cultures can be lighter than one
if the space between them is fluid,
like wind, or light between two open hands,
or the future, which knows how to change.

She's standing at the podium, waiting.
She wants to read a poem about climbing
a mountain. It's the song of what travelers
take with them, leave behind, transform.
From stillness, words ripple: clear cadence.

CLAIMS

I am not soft, hennaed hands,
a seduction of coral lips;
not the enticement of jasmine musk
through a tent flap at night;
not a swirl of sequined hips,
a glint of eyes unveiled.
I am neither harem's promise
nor desire's fulfillment.

I am not a shapeless peasant
trailing children like flies;
not a second wife, concubine,
kitchen drudge, house slave;
not foul-smelling, moth-eaten, primitive,
tent-dweller, grass-eater, rag-wearer.
I am neither a victim
nor an anachronism.

I am not a camel jockey, sand nigger, terrorist,
oil-rich, bloodthirsty, fiendish;
not a pawn of politicians,
nor a fanatic seeking violent heaven.
I am neither the mirror of your hatred and fear,
nor the reflection of your pity and scorn.
I have learned the world's histories,
and mine are among them.
My hands are open and empty:
the weapon you place in them is your own.

*

I am the woman remembering jasmine,
bougainvillea against chipped white stone.
I am the laboring farmwife
whose cracked hands claim this soil.
I am the writer whose blacked-out words
are birds' wings, razored and shorn.
I am the lost one who flees,
and the lost one returning;
I am the dream, and the stillness,
and the keen of mourning.

I am the wheat stalk, and I am
the olive. I am plowed fields young
with the music of crickets,
I am ancient earth struggling
to bear history's fruit.
I am the shift of soil
where green thrusts through,
and I am the furrow
embracing the seed again.

I am many rivulets watering
a tree, and I am the tree.
I am opposite banks of a river,
and I am the bridge.
I am light shimmering
off water at night,
and I am the dark sheen
that swallows the moon whole.

I am neither the end of the world
nor the beginning.

⇥ V ⇤

THE CHILD

swoops and turns
sea creature, dancer
ripple in an inland lake

palm floating on my belly
I wait for the world to open
for the swimmer to crest

breathe the morning—
dew-curled limbs
arcing toward light

FIRST YEAR

1.

I shuck myself of child,
drift unanchored
into the blue of evening

a marrowed twig
a bell chimed
to silence

(trees bend beneath the ripening flare
of autumn: horizon of winter
glinting down)

2.

at birth
the last dregs of river light
pooled in her night-flared eyes

music charted
the widening space
between us

Jerusalem in My Heart
a fierce opening
into sound

3.

in her face
three countries speak:
inflection

of olive
wheat
oregano

already she finds the cat
in two languages
knows the name of love

in three tongues
soon syllables will fall from her lips
the first rain

4.

now trees ignite again
she runs
a twist of motion

unsteady
through the bright chill day
turns at my voice

freeze-frame! I want to shout

before light moves on and over
before autumn breeze
yanks her

forward
into oncoming
weather

NURSING THE BABY

Although my mother might not have approved,
I nurse the baby well into toddlerhood.
I say it's a choice, but maybe I'm just too tired
to resist his frantic pleas: hands scrabbling
beneath shirt and bra, fabric thrust aside
till he reaches soft flesh, kneads it like a kitten,
latches to sweet reward with an audible sigh.
And who am I to argue—my own taut shoulders
releasing with each suckle, breath slowing
in pace with his as he surrenders, muscle by muscle,
swallow by milky swallow, to sleep?

Other times he approaches from the top,
thrusts his small head down my neckline,
body weight balanced on my hip
as I stand at the stove stirring oatmeal.
Perhaps he's a diver and my nipple a pearl,
a fisherman and my nightdress a net
filled with night's bounty—breasts flopping
like silvery fish, one hauled from its mooring,
succulent prize scooped greedily up and out.

To critics, I protest we're weaning,
it simply takes time. In public I snatch his hand back,
distract him with crackers and toys, feign strictness.
But when he tilts his eager face to mine,
inquiring gently, hopefully, *balla?* (my breasts
the prototype of roundness in his young life)
in a tone so seriously sweet nothing in me
is equal to the challenge, what can I do
but snuggle his body closer to mine, press my lips
to the crown of his head, raise my shirt
and offer the heavy globules, sweet and warm,
a world of love at his lips.

BURIED TREASURE

In the morning, we hoist ourselves up
hand over hand. The rope
is a twist of fiber about to snap.
Below us, the dark well of broken nights.

We say we have never been this tired
before. We'll say it tomorrow too.
Then we'll climb up the rope again.
Above us the baby will be clapping his hands

and chortling. Maybe we look like monkeys
in the zoo. Maybe we look like clowns.
When we get to the top we'll pull ourselves
over the ledge. We'll take a breath

and start spouting perky tunes.
We'll build towers, juggle balls,
wipe up a thousand spills.
Then we'll fall into the well again.

He thinks it's a game, how the adults
keep lying down. He crawls on us
and laughs, poking our eyes open
as if checking for buried treasure.

Even when his breathing slows at last
to silvery lift and fall
his dreaming eyelids quiver.
Perhaps a single brown rabbit

is hopping across a field,
or the sun has braided a ladder
to the sky, or a million poppies
with funny hats are waving hello.

PENGUIN PARENTS

As I watched the penguin parents
pass the fragile egg between them
in their brittle ballet, orb balanced
on awkward feet, tucked quickly
beneath paternal skin-flap

lest cold claim the beating life,
I recalled tending my son
after his break from mother-flesh—
how I curved my cramped arms, sloping breasts,
soft flab of stomach gone slack

around his frail unsheltered form,
baby heart beating against mine—
and I marveled at those stalwart standers
starving for months in Antarctic climes,
pecking the frigid air for snow,

nesting their warmth round their unborn chick.
How long could I fast? What extremities
of weather endure, what torments withstand
to protect my fragile offspring's life?
Am I really worth a parent's salt?

After egg birth the penguin mother,
weakened and desperate with hunger,
rolls the unhatched orb to her mate,
then makes her way to the frigid sea to feed.
Offspring are sheltered, but the parents must live.

I tuck my child beneath my breasts, ready
to face any danger in his defense, endure icescapes
of hunger, tundras of broken nights—
till my mate returns, scoops up the child,
and sends me staggering to the sea of sleep.

MY DAUGHTER ASKS ME WHAT THE SOUL IS

I who have no certainty of belief,
how can I answer? Maybe the soul
is a small bird inside the chest,
beating its wings for the joy of freedom.
Maybe it's a kernel of light, a pulsating star,
a small moon within us that waxes and wanes
without leaving the sky. Perhaps it's the energy
that lightens our steps, the radiance that illumines
our words, the sound that hums below everything.

I ponder the rush of water in the kitchen sink
as I wash, she dries. Her towel moves meditatively
across the flat white plates, the chipped soup bowls,
the forks bent from the garbage disposal.
Her hair is in need of brushing, her face slightly grubby,
her eyes luminous with thought. Gazing at her
I feel my soul, whatever that may be, expand.

Perhaps the olive trees outside the window
know the answer. They lean toward each other,
a bulwark against grayness: each tree its own life,
a witness to the sky, the sky a witness
to the trees, sky and trees a witness to the earth.
I turn off the water and dry my hands,
sense quiet vibrating like a pulse. Beneath my feet
the earth turns, its subtle motion a witness
to our humanness: so ordinary, so transcendent.

ANSWERS

What I carry with me?
Secrets. Peppermints. The smell of rain.

What I remember?
Specks of ash on a warm baked egg.

What I know?
How many songs till bedtime.

What I forget?
The exact color of my grandmother's eyes.

What I left behind?
Light on the river the morning you were born.

What I learned yesterday?
How to dance a jig barefoot, with blisters.

Where I'm going tomorrow?
With you, to a place where poppies bloom like days.

❧ VI ❧

POINTS OF DEPARTURE

Once a boy paddled a kayak
in the wrong direction.

He knew it was the Red Sea
all the way from Aqaba to Eilat.
He knew if you drew a line in water
it would vanish. He'd seen
how mountains map the sky,
brown swirls of smoke
etching the bowl of heat.

He never heard the sentry's
warning shot, his family's spiraling cries.

He was watching how sea met sky
and claimed it.
How there were no boundaries
but the shifting colors of blue
bitter and uncontainable.

*

Now they've opened a point of crossing.
After barbed wire, guns,
the jagged words,
sentries exchange cigarettes,
wave travelers through.

But the people waiting in line are tourists,
wear hats, sunscreen,
clutch passports in any color but native.

*

To cross, you need documentation, proof.

A man has been waiting years in the vacancy
between borders.

He wanders corridors, sleeps on hard benches,
wearied by each day's lengthening silence,
the border's depth and breadth

sifts memories

olives dense with drought

*

Where travelers pass
a girl watches, eyes like a sheath
bearing the sun's keen blade.

Sky rims the curve of ocean
opaque as the mountains
mapping the colors of salt.

I have lost track—what day was it when I arrrived in this land of earthen hills rising barricaded with stones to an unutterably crisp sky? When I saw the green slope of *Jabal* Abu-Ghneim for the first time? When I felt the rain close around me, dark as the long hours waiting for the news to change—though nothing changes but the details: the number of those stripped of their ID's, the number of stone-throwers, the number of wounded. Sahar says, we will never go back to the days of the *intifada*. Bassem disagrees. It will only get worse, he says; protests will spread through the towns like fire. When the first one is killed, you will see. Rana says, what kind of life can young people have here? We can think of nothing but our troubles, the political situation. At our age we should be thinking of philosophy, of love, of our futures. Here we have no future. Anne says, the psychiatrist they brought in to advise us on stress management told us to leave the country every few months, take a vacation, decompress. Meanwhile, Palestinians can't even go to Jerusalem, can't move from town to town. Daoud says, the oppression fills all available space in your brain, until finally the last bit of news sends you over the edge. Nihad asks me, are you Palestinian or American? I have Palestine in my heart, I reply, though I don't have the language. Ah, he replies, to say such a thing you are more Palestinian than most. We are tired, here. We have lost our passion.

The waiter brings *hummus*, *mtabal*, many kinds of salads. The waiter brings trays of *kebab* and *kefta*, baskets of stone-baked bread, platters of oranges and bananas. There is a fire building heat within the thick stone walls of this place. There are many voices weaving a cloth that wraps around me, a garment to wear against the cold. Outside, there are hills laced with enough stone to last a century, cropping through the soil of Palestine like a million broken teeth. There is a road littered with stones, lined with boys whose faces beneath their *kafiyyehs* are hard and vulnerable. They clench rocks in their fists; they shout at us, *'itla'a*, leave quickly. Who could live in a land so steeped in stone and not bend down for a chunk, lime edges cutting deep into the palm's soft flesh? Who could go year after year, knowing that just beyond that checkpoint are people who would like you to disappear, without thinking: I am not made of stone, I cannot bear this one more day! Who could be surprised at the way the flames from burning tires spurt orange, fierce against the clarity of the day, the dusky pallor of rapidly descending night?

West Bank, March 1997

JERUSALEM

In the Old City, grocers scoop rice and wheat
from huge sacks, pour grain into deep brass scales,
measure anise and cardamom and thyme.

When sun slips into the pans it's swept up
without charge, the way you don't pay for the fragrance
of coffee, *za'atar's* bright swirl of sumac.

Not like the mass of sorrow
weighting the air beneath the odor of cumin,
that tips the scales in every reckoning.

RAIN

*

Fragments of bone stuck to balconies
the word made flesh
breath splintered like shrapnel

impossible to speak beyond the bodies

*

how a word transforms us
seedling taking delicate hold
or a weed choking the tender plants

news enters us and puts down roots

*

we plant grief
drench it with our tears
it will not grow

*

the dead can't shield themselves
the useless petals of their hands

outflung hands

*

what weapon
can silence a million birds
crying at dawn for the sun?

*

we have unlearned how to speak to one another
torn to flesh, what words can mend us?

you cry, give us peace!
we cry, give us our lives!

peace grows like any other plant, on the land
it needs earth and water

*

our words flower from fragile bodies
sway on slender stalks
mouths tilted upward for the rain

FIFTY YEARS ON / STONES IN AN UNFINISHED WALL

For Palestine

I.

Fifty years on
I am trying to tell the story
of what was lost
before my birth

the story of what was there

before the stone house fell
        mortar blasted loose
        rocks carted away for new purposes, or smashed
        the land declared clean, empty

before the orange trees bowed in grief
blossoms sifting to the ground like snow
quickly melting

before my father clamped his teeth
    hard
        on the pit of exile
slammed shut the door to his eyes

before tears turned to disbelief
disbelief to anguish
anguish to helplessness
helplessness to rage
rage to despair

before the cup was filled
raised forcibly to our lips

fifty years on
    I am trying to tell the story
    of what we are still losing

2.

I am trying to find a home in history
but there is no more space in the books
for exiles

the arbiters of justice
have no time
for the dispossessed
without credentials

and what good are words
when there is no page
for the story?

3.

  the aftersong filters down
  like memory
        echo of ash

history erased the names
of four hundred eighteen villages
emptied, razed

but cactus still rims the perimeters
emblem of what will not stay hidden

In the Jaffa district alone:

Al-'Abbasiyya
Abu Kishk
Bayt Dajan
Biyar 'Adas
Fajja
Al-Haram
Ijlil al-Qibliyya
Ijlil al-Shamaliyya
al-Jammasin al-Gharbi
al-Jammasin al-Sharqi
Jarisha
Kafr 'Ana
al-Khayriyya
al-Mas'udiyya
al-Mirr
al-Muwaylih
Ranitya
al-Safiriyya
Salama
Saqiya
al-Sawalima
al-Shaykh Muwannis
Yazur

all that remains
a scattering of stones and rubble
across a forgotten landscape

fifty years on
the words push through

a splintered song
forced out one note
at a time

4.

The immensity of loss
shrouds everything

in despair
we seek the particular

light angling
in single rays

> *the houses of Dayr Yasin*
> *were built of stone, strongly built*
> *with thick walls*

> *a girls' school   a boys' school   a bakery*
> *two guest-houses   a social club*
> *three shops   four wells   two mosques*

a village of stone cutters
a village of teachers and shopkeepers

an ordinary village
with a peaceful reputation

until the massacre

> *carried out without discriminating*
> *among men and women*
> *children and old people*

in the aftermath
light remembers

light searches out the hidden places
fills every crevice

light peers through windows
slides across neatly swept doorsteps
finds the hiding places of the children

light slips into every place
where the villagers were killed
     the houses, the streets, the doorways
light traces the bloodstains

light glints off the trucks
that carried the men through the streets
like sheep before butchering

light pours into the wells
where they threw the bodies

light seeks out the places where sound
was silenced

light streams across stone
light stops at the quarry

5.

near Qisraya, circa 1938
a fisherman leans forward
flings his net
across a sea slightly stirred
by wind

to his left
land tumbles
rocky   blurred
to his right
sky is hemmed

by an unclear
horizon

(ten years
before the *Nakbeh*—

the future
already closing
down)

6.

fifty years later
shock still hollows the throats
of those driven out

> *without water, we stumbled into the hills*

> *a small child lay beside the road*
> *sucking the breast of its dead mother*

> *outside Lydda*
> *soldiers ordered everyone*
> *to throw all valuables onto a blanket*

> *one young man refused*

> *almost casually,*
> *the soldier pulled up his rifle*
> *shot the man*

> *he fell, bleeding and dying*
> *his bride screamed and cried*

he fell to the earth
they fell in despair to the earth

the earth held them
the earth soaked up their cries

their cries sank into the soil
filtered into underground streams

fifty springs on
their voices still rise from the earth

fierce as the poppies
that cry from the hills each spring

in remembrance

7.

some stories are told in passing
barely heard in the larger anguish

among those forced out
was a mother with two babies

one named Yasmine
and another
whose name no one remembers
her life so short
even its echo
is forgotten

the nameless child died on the march

it was a time of panic
no one could save a small girl
and so her face crumpled
lost beneath the weight of earth

I know only that she loved the moon
that lying ill on her mother's lap
she cried inconsolably
wanted to hold it in her hands

a child
she didn't know Palestine
would soon shine
    unreachable
  as the moon

8.

the river floods its banks
littering the troubled landscape

we pick our way amid shards
heir to a generation
    that broke their teeth on the bread of exile
    that cracked their hearts on the stone of exile
    necks bent beneath iron keys to absent doors

their lamentations
an unhealed wound

    I was forced to leave my village
    but the village refused to abandon me
      my blood is there
      my soul is flying in the sky over the old streets

fifty years on
    soul still seeks a sky

9.

the walls were torn down long ago
homes demolished
rebuilding forbidden

but the stones remain

someone dug them from the soil
with bare hands
carried them across the fields

someone set the stones
in place on the terraced slope

someone planted trees,
dug wells

someone still waits in the fields all night
humming the old songs quietly

someone watches stars chip darkness
into dawn

someone remembers
how stone holds dew through the summer night

how stone
waits for the thirsty birds

JERUSALEM SONG

Your walls fold gently,
a wingspan
embracing the dreaming city.

Your air drifts with the odor of incense,
women's voices floating upwards,
a twist of prayer toward heaven's ear.

I hold your name beneath my tongue
like a seed
slipped into the mouth for safekeeping.

Jerusalem, fold me like a handkerchief
into your bosom. I am
one word in a lover's letter,

a chip of blue tile in your sky.
Even those who have never seen you
walk your streets at night.

We wipe your dust from our feet
each morning, rise from our beds
wearied by the long distances

we have traveled to reach you.
See how we save even the broken bits
of pottery, fitting fragments together

along jagged lines to remember you.
Jerusalem, we are fledglings
crying for a nest.

THESE WORDS

These words are for Rana—
eighteen years old, a girl,
a wife, in Qur village,

Tulkarem, West Bank,
occupied Palestine.
Rana knew where she lived

and had no need for maps.
Did she hum quietly
to the child in her belly,

tremble when artillery pounded
the streets, when planes rained fire—
cries shaking the air,

men bearing another body past her door
for burial? These words
are for Rana—

pregnant, in labor, afraid—
and for the child
stirring in her womb,

rocked on an inland lake
of love.
Rana sought medicine, doctors.

Turned back at the checkpoint
by soldiers indifferent
to fear, or love,

or the fierce labor
of life, she found
only barricades, guns.

These words are for her desperate pleas,
for the pains coming fast, faster,
for the baby that entered the world

to breathe, then die.
These words are for Rana,
taken once more to the checkpoint,

once more turned back,
arriving at last at the hospital
already dead.

These words are for the family
expecting a birth
who bore their daughter and grandchild

to the burial place.
And these words are for their people
whose keening circles the globe

and is not heard.
These words are for you, and me,
for the lives we cherish,

the children we nurture,
the dailiness we claim, the griefs
we prefer not to see.

These words are the weight
cupped in our palms:
the small broken note of freedom.

And these words are for our silence.

THIS IS NOT A MASSACRE

What kind of war is this?
      —Amira Hass, *Ha'aretz*, April 19, 2002.

This is a humanitarian operation.
All efforts have been made to protect
civilians. Homes demolished
above the heads of owners
ensure the absence of booby-traps.
Surely the dead must realize
that this operation saved lives.

Our task is damage control.
Keep out the medical teams.
Let the voices beneath the rubble
fade away. Keep out the Red Cross,
the ambulances, the international observers,
the civilians bearing food and water.
Mercy has no place in the "city of bombers."

Extermination of vipers' nests
requires absolute precision.
Ignore the survivors
searching through ruins for shards
of their lives: a plate, a shoe,
a cup, a sack of rice. Ignore
the strewn body parts,
the leg twisted yards away
from the white and bloated hand,
the boys cradling a small charred foot.
Dismembered bodies
cannot remember themselves.

What remains? Only traces.
That photo (dead girl,
hand clutched at her side,
once-white ribbon still discernible
on her pallid profile,
ashen skin melting into the dust
that clogs her mouth)
nothing more than shadow
of the drowned, odor of mint
wafting from a grave.

Say it fast over and over:
this is not a massacre this
is not a massacre this is not
a massacre this is not a
massacre this is not
a massacre this is not a
massacre

For the people of Jenin, Palestine

RACHEL CORRIE

Whatever words might have been adequate
have become a high, fluted cry

like the keening *whit-tu-tu*
of the unseen bird outside

my window. All day I have been trying
to break free from the bulldozer's

blade, piled earth, steel treads fracturing
skull and chest, that moment of protest,

stilled frame reverberating
beyond the moment, like the kid

in Tiananmen Square before the tank.
Rachel's bright orange jacket

and megaphone.
Her kind and tired eyes.

All day I have been pierced
by the high note of helplessness,

the ragged beat of despair.
Shrouded body with its blur of blood.

The quiet hands of mourners
bearing her, flag-sheathed, across the town.

*

And why was she there?
Ask the ones whose truths she saw

and sought to speak. Ask the child
slumped atop concrete slabs—

debris of his demolished home.
Ask the pregnant woman

trapped under crushing rubble
cradling a toddler while she died.

Ask the families
huddled in wind-ripped tents,

homes wrecked without warning
to make way for the separation wall.

*

Whatever words we have are useless
against this cruel weight. The bird's cry

keens from every crack in the edifice
of history. Before she died, Rachel Corrie wrote,

"I have a home.
I am allowed to go see the ocean."

In memory of Rachel Corrie, 23 years old, member of the
International Solidarity Movement, killed by an Israeli
bulldozer while trying to prevent demolition of a Pales-
tinian family's house.

SHARDS

A technical failure   terrible accident   unfortunate
event   regrettable but necessary   we had
to take action   there was no choice

Excuses pile up like body parts (gaping yellow-toothed
jaw separated from its head, neck slit open below the absent
chin, burned torso flaking like singed paper, brain spilling
from a broken child-size skull, severed hand still grasping).

Parts don't make a whole.
Aid workers collecting heads and hands from the street in black
garbage bags lay out decapitated bodies on silver morgue trays, stack
appendages beside them like missing puzzle pieces, then go home
and hold their heads in their hands.

Maybe they pray for amnesia. Maybe they search
for answers: how many hands it takes to staunch a wound that won't
stop bleeding, how to remember the dream of an ordinary
life. Can a headless handless body cradle a child, greet
a neighbor, plant an orchard, plow a field, sign a peace treaty?

Some of the dead kept their heads. One young mother lies
waxen, holding two children in rigid embrace, slumbering portrait
belied by the blood smearing their cheeks—infant's mouth
slightly open, as if dreaming of a breast, the warm flow of milk;
tousle-haired girl-child turning in death's dream.

Part of this has been screamed a million times.
Part of it will never be heard.
Part of it reflects like quiet light off the streams of untreated sewage
and pools of shimmering blood in Gaza lanes.

Part of it hides behind the headlines
where this shard of the story will never be told.

Beit Hanoun, November 2006

CYCLONES AND SEEDS

Headlines declare retaliations,
military strikes. In the lanes
kids bleed in the dust
while soldiers bar the way
to ambulances: no passage for mercy.

Love is in the details.
I want to know what that man,
twenty-five years old,
killed at his window
cradling his daughter in his arms,
ate for breakfast.
How many years of saving,
one dinar at a time,
it took to build that pile of rubble
that was once a home.
If the boy killed by a sniper
on his way to school
argued with his mother that morning.
If the pregnant woman shot at the checkpoint
was afraid of labor, anemic;
what she felt when her infant
turned beneath her heart.
What that stillborn child might have been named
if its desperate mother
had gotten through to the hospital
ringed with tanks.
Was it a girl? First born?
Fifth in a line of sons?

I want to save everything broken,
collect shards of crockery
from the rubble, gently blot the blood
from the gouged-up earth,

smooth the lashes that lie like tears
on the dead boys' cheeks.
I want to count the fingers and toes of each baby
before it's tucked into the earth.

I want the killers to look survivors in the eye,
taste the gore of the dead in their mouths,
lie down in the dirt with the corpses they've created
and remember their own history.
I want them to never sleep at night again.

I want the politicians brought before a line-up
Of one Palestinian child one Israeli child one Afghani child
One American child one Iraqi child one British child
(all little girls, age four, with neat pigtails,
scrubbed faces, large trusting eyes).
Let them choose the child with the greatest value.

I want the headlines to scream
of Samer Suleiman Abu Mayaleh
fourteen years old   stripped
pushed face down in the street

soldiers fired one bullet at close range
up his rectum
it burned through his body
penetrating liver, heart
blood soaking the dust
from veins three quarters drained

they said a heart attack killed the boy

don't tell me you believe them
that you hadn't heard

that you're too busy to protest
that you couldn't do anything anyway
that the powers-that-be never listen

so what if we're shouting into a storm
if wind swallows words like rain
it takes just a single voice to break the silence

the world turns in the night
voices planted in darkness
still spark the wounded earth to light

freedom is a seed a plant a prayer a chant a cyclone

it grows in hard places
courses through the bones
like light a song a sound a voice
a river of voices
bearing us forward

winged seeds upon the storm

VII

NO

There's no poetry in it,
but I need to say something about No,
how it stands up, no matter how unpopular,
in the face of injustice. Maybe it can't
thwart history: the powerful have always known
what they can do, and they do it.
No can't stop an avalanche.
But No could be a retaining wall
built of rough stones wrested from the earth,
carried one by one up the hill on someone's back.
No might be a tree in the middle of a village street:
traffic shifts to flow around it, its presence
a reminder of what used to be, what won't be
forgotten. No is the perimeter of stubborn cactus
springing up around destroyed villages.
You can bulldoze houses, evict or kill the inhabitants,
but the thorns of memory can't be eliminated.
No is steadfast. It knows what it's like
to have nothing in its hands but dignity.

THE COFFIN MAKER SPEAKS

At first it was shocking—orders flooding in
faster than I could meet. I worked
through the nights, tried to ignore
the sound of planes overhead,
reverberations shaking my bones,
acid fear, the jagged weeping
of those who came to plead my services.
I focused on the saw in my hands,
burn of blisters, sweet smell of sawdust;
hoped that fatigue would push aside
my labor's purpose.

Wood fell scarce as the pile of coffins grew.
I sent my oldest son out for more,
but there was scant passage on the bombed out roads,
and those who could make it through
brought food for the living, not planks for the dead.
So I economized, cut more carefully than ever,
reworked the extra scraps.
It helped that so many coffins were child-sized.

I built the boxes well, nailed them strong,
loaded them on the waiting trucks,
did my job but could do no more.
When they urged me to the gravesite—
that long grieving gash in earth
echoing the sky's torn warplane wound—
I turned away, busied myself with my tools.
Let others lay the shrouded forms
in new-cut wood, lower the lidded boxes one by one
(stilled row of toppled dominos,
long line of broken teeth).
Let those who can bear it read the *Fatiha*
over the crushed and broken dead.

If I am to go on making coffins,
let me sleep without knowledge.

But what sleep have we in this flattened city?
My neighbors hung white flags on their cars
as they fled. Now they lie still and cold,
waiting to occupy my boxes. Tonight
I'll pull the white sheet—that useless plea
for mercy—from my window.
Better to save it for my shroud.

One day, *insha'allah,* I'll return
to woodwork for the living.
I'll build doors for every home in town,
smooth and strong and solid;
doors that will open quickly in times of danger,
let the desperate in for shelter.
I'll use oak, cherry, anything but pine.

For now, I do my work. Come to me
and I'll build you what you need.
Tell me the dimensions, the height or weight,
and I'll meet your specifications.
But keep the names and ages to yourself.
Already my dreams are jagged.
Let me not wake splintered from my sleep
crying for Fatima, Rafik, Soha, Hassan, Dalia,
or smoothing a newborn newdead infant's face.
Later I too will weep. But if you wish me
to house the homeless dead,
let me keep my nightmares nameless.

South Lebanon, 2006

A FEW REASONS TO OPPOSE THE WAR

because wind soughs in the branches of trees
like blood sighing through veins

because in each country there are songs
huddled like wet-feathered birds

because even though the news has nothing new to say
and keeps on saying it
NO still fights its way into the world

because for every bomb that is readied
a baby nestles into her mother
latches onto a nipple beaded with milk

because the tulips have waited all winter
in the cold dark earth

because each morning the wildflowers outside my window
raise their yellow faces to the sun

because we are all so helplessly in love
with the light

ASPHODEL

It rises from its stalk,
stamened tongue of March,
flaring across every wasteland or open space
—profusion of pink-white stars—
till air itself sparks with delight!

Asphodel: known to the ancients
as nourishment, circulatory medicine,
glue for the shoemakers.
Lovers pluck its blossoms,
trace the delicate map of its petals.
Young boys whittle its stalks into windmills.

Today, all other signs of spring—
butterflies trembling across a meadow,
kites breaking through blue air
toward a sea still thoughtful with the memory
of winter—are but echoes
of the land-flung asphodel
brimming its melody across the hills.

Here, on this green coastal slope,
before afternoon turns to night,
before tomorrow's dawn is darkened by news
of war, before armies ready their weapons,
before gravediggers whet their shovels
and parents prepare their tears,
let us remember the pliant asphodel:

how it rises from stony earth to joyous
air, how it carries its song so briefly,
so tenderly, so open to the light.

ARGUMENTS

consider the infinite fragility of an infant's skull
how the bones lie soft and open
only time knitting them shut

consider a delicate porcelain bowl—
how it crushes under a single blow
in one moment whole years disappear

consider: beneath the din of explosions
no voice can be heard
no cry

consider your own sky on fire
your name erased
your children's lives "a price worth paying"

consider the faces you do not see
the eyes you refuse to meet
collateral damage

how in these words
the world
cracks open

For the people of Iraq

COUNTDOWN

Glowering air, dazed
with Saharan dust, shrouds
the horizon. Wildflowers
huddle in the empty lots,
keep their heads tucked down,
their mouths snapped shut.

Yesterday we were a fingertip
from war. Today the distance is that
of a hangnail. I turn my hands over
and over, searching for some news
I can hold, but find only
calloused flesh, rough bitten skin.
Air cupped in my palms
feels heavier than grief.

My baby claps his chubby hands,
fingers splayed like stars.
He grips my forefinger fiercely
as if I were a rudder.

What love can save us now?
Outside the rain starts falling.

Next there is asphodel, anemone,
children gathering twigs
and tadpoles. Next there are kite tails
wandering over the wide sky
of spring. Next are hen's eggs
fresh-laid and almond trees breaking
to blossom and village bread fragrant
from dome-shaped ovens of clay
and kittens mewing and seasons uncurling
like new leaves, tender and green,
and next there is war.

Outside the U.S. embassy, barbed wire imprisons everything:
empty lot with its chant of wildflowers
tired shadows of olive trees, broken sky.

Memory flaps like a bat in the attic.
We've been here before: war and coffee,
full-color photos in the glossies.

Only this time they're calling them
"decapitation strikes."
Every war needs a bit of variety.

Low sun flares its crimson light
across the land. It will rise again tomorrow,
vigilant and weary as hope.

NIGHT SKY

I line the candles up in my window:
tall, short, fat, round, square.
Lit, the flames burn equally.

Outside, the sky holds constellations
I remember from childhood nights,
my mother's patient voice

directing my gaze. Big Dipper.
Little Dipper. Hunter Orion's belt.
They shine unchanged

over this divided capital
on a divided island
in our divided world.

Candles and stars
are easier than news.
Television announcers describe

the infinite variety
of bombs. One flattens everything
in a two-kilometer radius:

libraries, movie theaters, schools.
Another sucks up acres of oxygen,
suffocating cats, cows, children.

From Baghdad, Barbara writes of families
so desperate to get a child out
they stop any foreigner in the street.

She pleads, "Just imagine our lives."
Tilting my head to the night sky
I watch the stars shine calmly

over our small world.
From wherever we are,
Baghdad is not so far.

Nicosia, Cyprus

It's true, whatever we do or don't do may come to haunt us.
Outside a man walks by: blue shirt, bald head. He blends
into the dusk, like the olive tree outside my window,
the blue-gray sky washed clean by recent rain,
the bird whose twittering heralds the evening.
May we all fit together like this: trees, birds, sky,
people, separate elements in a living portrait,
outlines smoothed by the forgiving wash
of lingering light. Whatever the skins we live in,
the names we choose, the gods we claim or disavow,
may we be like grains of sand on the beach at night:
a hundred million separate particles
creating a single expanse on which to lie back
and study the stars. And may we remember the generosity
of light: how it travels through unimaginable darkness,
age after age, to light our small human night.

PRACTICING LOVING KINDNESS

Bless the maniac
barreling down the one-way street
the wrong way,
who shakes his fist when I honk.
May he live long enough
to take driving lessons.

Bless the postman
puffing under the no-smoking sign.
(When I complain, my mail
goes mysteriously missing
for months.) Bless all those
who debauch the air,
the mother wafting fumes
across her baby's carriage,
the man whose glowing stub
accosts a pregnant woman's face.
May they unlearn how to exhale.

Bless the politicians
who both give and receive
bribes and favors.
Bless the constituents
seeking personal gain,
the thieves, the liars, the sharks.
And bless the fools
who make corruption easy.
May they be spared
both wealth and penury.

Bless the soldiers guarding checkpoints
where women labor and give birth
in the dirt. Bless the settlers
swinging clubs into teenager's faces,

the boys shooting boys with bullets
aimed to kill, the men driving bulldozers
that flatten lives to rubble.
May they wake from the dream of power,
drenched in the cold sweat
of understanding. May they learn
the body's frailty, the immensity of the soul.

Bless the destroyers of Falluja,
the wreckers of Babylon,
the torturers of Abu Ghraib
and Guantanamo Bay.
May they understand desolation,
may they comprehend despair.

Bless the peace makers,
the teachers, the word-workers;
the wavers of flags
and the makers of fighter jets.
May they know the ends of their labor,
and the means. May they make
reparations. May they rebuild.

Bless this planet, so cudgeled,
so bounteous: the rain forests,
the tundra, the ozone layer.
May it persevere beyond
our human follies. May it bloom.

Bless cynicism. Bless hope.
Bless the fingers that type,
the computer that processes,
the printer that prints.
Bless email and snail mail.

Bless poetry books that cross oceans
in battered envelopes,
bearing small flames of words.

The epigraph by Cavafy opening the book is taken from the poem "Ithaka," in *The Poems of C. P. Cavafy*, translated by John Mavrogordato (NY, The Grove Press, 1952).

The italicized sections of "50 Years On/ Stones in an Unfinished Wall" are taken, in most cases verbatim, from various historical and journalistic sources, including Walid Khalidi's *All That Remains: The Palestinian Villages Occupied and Depopulated by Israel in 1948* (Washington D.C: Institute for Palestine Studies, 1992), the Deir Yassin OnLine Information Center (http://www.deiryassin.org), Father Audeh Rantisi's *Blessed are the Peacemakers: The History of a Palestinian Christian*, and Reuters news reports.

The phrase "a price worth paying" in "Arguments" refers to a statement by U.S. Secretary of State Madeline Albright in a 1996 interview with Lesley Stahl on CBS's *60 Minutes*. Stahl, asking Albright about the effects of sanctions on Iraq, said, "We have heard that half a million children have died. I mean, that's more children than died in Hiroshima. And, you know, is the price worth it?" Albright replied: "I think this is a very hard choice, but the price—we think the price is worth it."

"Shards" is based on descriptions by Jennifer Lowenstein in "Nightmares: How Gaza Offends Us All," published in *Palestine Internationalist*, Volume 2 Issue 4 (Jun 2007).

ACKNOWLEDGMENTS

I am grateful to more people than I can name here whose friendship, encouragement, critical advice, inspiration and literary example have helped make this book possible. I owe a great debt to Pauline Kaldas and David Williams, whose generosity, sensitivity and insight nurtured my literary efforts when I was still searching for a voice. My thanks to them and to Mona Fayad, Nathalie Handal, Joanna Kadi, Mohja Kahf, Deborah al-Najjar, Julie Olin-Ammentorp, Laura Porter and Therese Saliba for decades of friendship, support, literary critiques, and comradery in the word mills. Special thanks to Naomi Shihab Nye for inspiration and encouragement. My gratitude to Sue Dahdah and Diana Saleh Doakes for long ago encouraging my love of the written word, to Elaine Hagopian and Michael Suleiman for intellectual mentorship and ongoing support, to Elizabeth Quinlan and Jim Carlisle for literary companionship at a time I might otherwise have stopped writing, to Anya Achtenberg for inspiration and literary activism, and to Beverly Monestier for helping me recreate a literary life in Cyprus. I am immensely grateful to Samira Atallah and Souad Dajani for friendship at critical times. And to so many others who have buoyed my days and seen me across dark waters—thank you.

I am deeply saddened that some people to whom I owe gratitude are no longer here to see this book: Faris Bouhafa, whose zest for life energized me; Daria Donnelly, whose passion for poetry brightened so many conversations; Evelyn Menconi, who helped me find a home in the Boston Arab-American community; Haas Mroue, whose fierce words and gentle spirit accompanied me across many years; and Hilda Silverman, whose passion for justice and humanity continue to inspire me. I am diminished without them.

I am indebted to Flight of the Mind: Writing Workshops for Women, to Molly Fisk's online Poetry Boot Camp, and to The William Joiner Center for the Study of War and Social Consequences for inspiring workshop experiences.

Much gratitude to my family for the role they have played (sometimes unwittingly) in my literary endeavors. Thanks to Abla Majaj for her enthusiasm for my writing, and for being part of the tapestry of memory that informs these poems. Special thanks to Nadia and Nicolas Alexandrou-Majaj for bringing daily joy and inspiration to my life, as well as their own special kind of poetry. My greatest debt, unpayable, is to Andreas N. Alexandrou, who first introduced me to the words of the poet Constantine Cavafy, and who has shared my life's journey for almost three decades, opening doors I did not know were closed. For his insight, sensitivity, largesse of spirit, love and faithfulness across years and continents, I offer unbounded thanks.

These poems are in memory of my mother, Jean Caroline Stoltenberg Majaj, who taught me by example how literature deepens our humanity; my father, Isa Joudeh Majaj, who conveyed a passion for Palestine and for justice that informs my being; and my aunt, Marian Stoltenberg Jones Johnson, whose life exemplified the importance of the past to the present. Gone too soon, they will be remembered always.

PUBLICATION CREDITS:

I am grateful to the editors of the following journals and anthologies in which some of these poems first appeared, at times under different titles or in different versions: *Al Jadid,* for "Jerusalem" and "Arguments"; *Babel Fruit,* for "Night Sky"; *Banipal: Magazine of Modern Arab Literature,* for "Morning" and "Asphodel," *Cadences: A Journal of Literature and the Arts in Cyprus,* for "Reunion," "Provenance," "Grief Ghosts," "Practicing Loving Kindness," and "My Daughter Asks Me What the Soul Is"; *Café Solo,* for "Two Flutes" and "Seasons of Fire, Seasons of Light"; *Dance the Guns to Silence: 100 Poems for Ken Saro-Wiwa* (Flipped Eye Publishing, 2005), for "This is Not a Massacre"; *Et in Terra Pax* (En Tipis Publications, 2007), for "Doorway"; *Evergreen: The Evergreen Magazine,* for "Rachel Corrie"; *Food for our Grandmothers* (South End Press, 1994), for "Claims"; *Forkroads,* for "Tata Olga's Hands"; *International Feminist Journal of Politics,* for "Shards"; *Journal of the Asian American Renaissance,* for "Weave of Light"; *Literary Mama* (www.literarymama.com), for "Answers"; *Make/Shift: Feminisms in Motion,* for "Another Place"; *91st Meridian,* for "Asphodel"; *Mizna,* for "In Season," "Pomelo Days," These Words," and "Cyclones and Seeds"; *Mr. Cogito,* for "In Beirut" and "Tata Bahiyeh"; The New Verse News (www.newversenews.com), for "Out-of-State"; *Ordinary Time* (The Dedalus Press, 1999), for "Homemaking"; *The Other Voices International Project,* for "No" and "Living in History"; *Peaceworks,* for "Rain"; *Perihelion,* for "Warbreak" and "First Year"; *The Poetry of Arab Women* (Interlink, 2001), for "Jerusalem Song"; *Post-Gibran: Anthology of New Arab American Writing* (Jusoor 11/12; distributed by Syracuse University Press, 1999), for "Sea Bones," "Departure," and Poppies"; *Ripe Guava: Voices of Women of Color,* for "Fifty Years On/ Stones in an Unfinished Wall"; *Scheherazade's Legacy: Arab and Arab-American Women on Writing* (Greenwood/Praeger, 2004), for "What Comes Next," "Cadence" and "Countdown"; *The Spirit,* for "I Remember My Father's Hands," *The Thistle,* for "The Days" and "Taproot"; *Women Outdoors,* for "In the Woods"; *The Worcester Review,* for "Groundspace," *The Texas Observer,* for "Points of Departure"; *Unsettling America: An Anthology of Contemporary Multicultural Poetry* (Viking Penguin USA, 1994), for "Recognized Futures"; *Winning Writers* (www.winningwriters.com), for "It Wasn't Poetry" and "What She Said"; and *World Literature Today,* for "Stone Fence," "Olive Trees," "Origins" and "The Coffin Maker Speaks."

LISA SUHAIR MAJAJ, a Palestinian-American, grew up in Amman, Jordan, was educated in Beirut, Lebanon and Ann Arbor, Michigan, and lived in the U.S. for two decades before moving to Nicosia, Cyprus. She has read her poetry and prose across the U.S. and in Europe and the Middle East, and has published widely in journals such as *World Literature Today, South Atlantic Quarterly, Visions International, Perhihelion Review, Banipal: Magazine of Modern Arab Literature, Cadences: A Journal of Literature and the Arts in Cyprus, The Jerusalem Times* and elsewhere. She is also a longtime scholar of Arab-American literature. Her previous books include two chapbooks of poetry, *These Words* and *What She Said,* and three co-edited collections of literary essays: *Intersections: Gender, Nation and Community in Arab Women's Novels, Etel Adnan: Critical Essays on the Arab-American Writer and Artist,* and *Going Global: The Transnational Reception of Third World Women Writers.* She lives in Cyprus with her family.

DEL SOL PRESS, based out of Washington, D.C., publishes exemplary and edgy fiction, poetry, and nonfiction (mostly contemporary, with the occasional reprint). Founded in 2002, the press sponsors two annual competitions:

THE DEL SOL PRESS POETRY PRIZE is a yearly book-length competition with a January deadline for an unpublished book of poems.

THE ROBERT OLEN BUTLER FICTION PRIZE is awarded for the best short story, published or unpublished. The deadline is in November of each year.

http://webdelsol.com/dsp

CPSIA information can be obtained
at www.ICGtesting.com
Printed in the USA
LVHW080458060422
715460LV00008B/307